A Touch of the Soul

Katie Baines

BookLeaf
Publishing

India | USA | UK

Presentation by *BookLeaf Publishing*

Web: www.bookleafpub.com

E-mail: info@bookleafpub.com

ISBN: 978-93-5761-243-2

First edition 2022

DEDICATION

To my Dad George, your generous heart will forever touch my soul.

ACKNOWLEDGEMENT

I would like to thank my biological family and Christian family and friends for encouraging me through the highs and lows of life. In particular, I am thankful to my Mum, Nan and my late father who all saw something special in me and inspired me to do the things in life that I love and am passionate about. A special thanks of gratitude to my personal tutor, dissertation supervisor and friend Suganthi John. A person who praised my ability to write from the moment I stepped foot at the University of Birmingham. Not forgetting God. I am so grateful for the gift of words that he has given me.

PREFACE

I felt prompted by God to share my love of words and my love of him. I found God two and a half years ago in one of my darkest places. My life has been transformed by knowing Jesus, and I wanted to demonstrate my experience of God's healing and love through the hardships we face in life through poetry. I have faced difficulties with my mental health, loneliness and losing my Dad. I wanted to encourage others to know that there is a God that exists to give you unconditional love. To bless people with the beauty of words is important to me and I hope and pray that this book does exactly that.

Peace

A waterfall trickling
The sweet sound of birdsong
Wind chimes dancing
Your favourite song murmuring

For us,
Peace comes in differing forms
An experience
Relaxing you

But you father give me…

A calmness
A stillness
A feeling
Quiet

My father
I thank you
I praise you
For the peace that fills my heart

On days where I am tangled in chaos
When my day feels like a rollercoaster
Emotions running high
Your peace falls upon me

When grief comes to the forefront
Where rejection burns
When life hurts
Your peace is all I need

Greater than any sound I could hear
You touch my soul
Hold me close
With your perfect peace

A Peace in my Heart

As I child I'd look up to the clouds
I'd see white puffy shapes of fun
Joy filled my heart

As I grew older
Dark clouds lay heavy on my heart
A sadness hanging over me

War was on the cards
Pulled from pillar to post
Joy to sadness
Sadness to joy

There were two of me
bubbly , life of the party, full of energy
Contrasted with
a girl filled with depression and darkness

I didn't understand
Two sides of the coin
Glass full
Glass empty

Medication after medication
Therapist after therapist
Trapped in a whirlwind of emotions

Why me?
Why am I like this?
Why can't I be normal?

Then Jesus came
He greeted me at a time of despair
He filled my heart with peace

A peace surpassing all understanding
An acceptance of who I am
I finally felt wanted

He created me to be me
Not tied down with societies expectations
Not to feel abnormal
Not defined by contrasting moods

He gave me a peace in my heart
A comfort that no one else could give
An understanding of who I am

So here I am
Thankful for life
Thankful that I am here
Proud to be me

Agape

Love is all around us
In many ways for us to see
But there's only so much love the Earth can
offer

What we truly need is life
To be alive and living
To be loved unconditionally

Our hearts yearn for more
For more love and life
There's only one place to go
His arms are wide open
Ready and waiting
Like a father
awaiting his first touch of his child

The love we ache for
The life we are desperate to know
It's right there in front of us

Some days we are blind
Some days we are asleep
But his love never waivers

It may seem complicated but
The answer is clear
Lord, Jesus Christ

An Overfilled Closet

A closet
Filled with my troubles
Packed with emotions and my past

I open the door
Overwhelmed by the mess
I have two choices

I shut it struggling to close the door
Or
I take one piece out

One part of my past
I hold it
It's just one piece to hold

I hear his voice
Just one thing at a time

I hold my arms out
My hands are met by Jesus

He takes it
With open arms

My child he says
Let's work this out together

I put on my dress
It's now beautifully white
Pure and clean
For I am cleansed of my unrighteousness

I smile joyfully
Touched by the spirit

A new day
A Fresh start
A new beginning

I'm ready to go
Ready to experience the grace of God
He has arrived
I am walking with him out of darkness

You are not alone

Past hurt may arise
Difficult memories may resurface
But hold on to me
You are not alone

Every storm you face
I am by your side
Holding your hand tightly
You are not alone

I am your friend
Your father
And your all loving creator
You are not alone

You are made in my image
Created in my likeness
You are truly beautiful
You are not alone

Your worries
Your fears
Cast them on to to me
You are not alone

I will protect you
I will heal you
I will love you
You are not alone

You are my child
I delight in you
And you will forever be mine
You are not alone

Endless Searching

My world is tumbling down
I'm out of control
I fear so much
I'm searching for something
Searching for peace

Surrounded by love
Encouraged by many
Held up by friends
Affirmations to keep me strong
Yet I'm still searching

The storms test me
The temptation finds me
The anger builds up
The hurt and tears
Still searching

When will I know what I'm searching for ?
When will this be over ?
So many questions
So many doubts
Starting to detest me

The truth tells me all I need is you
Yet I feel so lonely even knowing you're there
I'm clinging on
My hands feel like they are slipping
Hold on to them Lord

Don't let me fall
Even though it feels like I've already hit the
ground
Help me Abba
Pick me up and spin me around
Like a father does with his child

Your word keeps me going
My prayers will never fail
I hold on to your truth
I'll never stop believing
I won't stop loving you

Abba's Virtues

Oh come let us adore him
In the spirit of light
Let him place his hands upon you
And let his grace be known

Kindness and Gentleness
Adoration and love
Comfort and grace
Wisdom and more

Oh to be sinners
In a world full of earthly desires
We just need his love
His beautiful Love

We don't deserve his grace
Or his mercy
Yet God is here
A gentle wind in the midst of a storm

Life isn't easy
But God never promised it would be so
The dark trials will test us
But we are not alone

You see Jesus is here
Our guiding friend
Holding our hand
As we walk out of darkness

Oh how blessed are we;
To know the goodness of God
Let's love him eternally
Just as he does for us

Life

You gave us life
We don't always feel grateful
We forget the cross
But life
You gave us life

Darkness surrounds us
At times it seems pitch black
Darker than the midnight sky
Stars come peeping through
Just like those stars
You shine

You are our light in the darkness
You see everything
You see the picture clearer than we do
When our eyes are shut
You can open them
Open them for us to see the way to your
gleaming kingdom

We have a purpose
We aren't here merely by chance
There's a reason why you chose us

A reason I'm writing this now

You never fail us
You never leave us alone in the gloom
You fight for us
When we can't stand up
You lift us, without us realising;
You've been carrying us all along

Our footprints are not two
But they are four
Yours and mine
You trek along with us
You go before us
And when we can't walk anymore
You always pick your children up

Life
You gave us life
Let's be thankful
Keep rooted to the cross
Life
You gave us life

The Thief of Joy

Comparison is the thief of joy
Someone once told me
Yet we still compare
Wishing we were someone else

Looking at others lives
With rose coloured glasses
We forget
Everyone is facing trials

God made you and I unique
He made our lives different
He showers us with an abundance of pleasure
In distinct ways to us all

My path is different than yours
Your path is different to mine
Our blessings are individual to us
Jesus made it so

As hard as it may be
We should praise
Keep our faith strong
Because a blessing is floating our way

Comparison is the thief of joy
Someone once told me
I want to keep hold of my joy
As my joy is unique to me

God's Grace

Gracious and faithful
That's who you are God

You draw near to us
Even when we fall

We veer off into wrong directions
Tiptoe on the paths that are not of you

But you arrive just in time
Everything in your time is perfect

You are waiting on the path you chose
Waving joyfully
Inviting us back to you

You wipe away our tears
As we wail for forgiveness

Like a flick of a switch
All is forgiven

And Grace,
Grace shines upon us

A blessing we don't deserve
But a blessing God desires to give us

Next time you wander down a different path
Be reminded of the gentle whisper
The words from your father that echo in your ear

It's never too late to turn round
And skip in delight back towards your father

His grace is never ending
Accept it with a smile

Flower

Like a flower
We grow and flourish
We try to reach higher

We start small
Desperate for water
And growth

Eventually,
We are full of colour and scent
And can brighten people's days
But only with Jesus

Flowers didn't appear
From thin air
They were created

Like a flower
You were created
You are here for a purpose

Beautifully sculpted
Unique
And special

These are truths from our father
If only we could see ourselves as he does
Our perspective would change

He created you for a reason
Trust in that
And let the lord teach you to flower

Put your growth in his hands
Like a farmer does with his crops
And Let his colour shine through you

Outrageously Loved

You are loved
Has anyone ever told you that ?
Have you ever felt warmth and adoration from
someone?
A fuzzy feeling in your tummy

For what I am about to tell you
Is beautiful
The lord
He loves you

He knows you
He sees you
He is proud of you
Proud of his creation in you

Hear this
He loved you before you were in womb
Before you took your first breath
He loved you when he chose you to be his child

Nothing can disconnect us from his love
It's there
Always
And forever

In life we can feel lonely
Isolated
But take heart dear friends
You are outrageously loved

I give it to you Lord

I am broken
I am torn
The pain I feel, the loss
It feels too much to bear

I am scared
I am lonely
I feel forgotten
And I am lost

I feel you reaching out to me
Calling my name
Yet sometimes I am blind to see
Caught up in the hurricane

I am too proud
And perhaps too stubborn
You want me to give it you
Yet it feels so hard

I am reminded of your gentleness
Your warm heart.
You want to take away my pain
You long to carry me

I must let my guard down
Let you pour out your love
And allow the spirit to wash over me
Oh Jesus how I need you

I ask you now in your name
To heal me
And to take away my burdens
I give it to you Lord

Your Beauty

When I wake in the morning,
I look to the sky
I'm reminded of the beauty
The world you created

Every leaf that has fallen
The intricacies
The detail
You made them unique

Like a leaf
I sometimes fall
But there's hope in each season
as those leaves return to their trees

Heavenliness surrounds us
Yet we sometimes forget
Everything you have made
For your children

Your creation is majestic
You are flawless
The details of the earth
We should not take for granted

As I walk with you
I will be in awe of your beauty
Thankful for the earth
And thankful for you

A hole in your heart

Who knew that love would hurt?
You hear it in tv, films and even in passing
It is true
Love hurts

You lose a part of you
When you lose a loved one
The pain at times: unbearable
An ache in your heart that you can't explain

A burning sensation of fear
Tears flow uncontrollably
A screaming inside you
A hole left in your heart

It can seem that no one understands
You feel alone in a bush of thorns
Continually pricking you
And pushing you down

Someone sees you
Sees your anguish
Sees your breaking heart
And that's Jesus

Remember Lazarus' death
Jesus wept
And just like he did then
He weeps with us

He sees our mourning
Our cries at night when we feel abandoned
He holds us tight
Comforting us through the storm

Grief is unique and personal to each of us
It's a part of life
But there's joy to come
A peace that surpasses all understanding

Take hope dear friends
That you are not alone in your sorrow
There's a hand reaching out to you
Take it

Do not be afraid to let Jesus in
He longs to be the blanket wrapped around you
when you feel cold
He wants to help you
And he will heal the hole in your heart

My Umbrella

When I was a child
I danced with my umbrella in the rain
Happy to be outside

I'd stomp in the puddles
Loving the weather
The joy it brought

As I grew older
I started to detest the rain
Desperate for sunnier days

When a storm now hits
I take shelter
I try to keep warm

You see recently,
I realised
The protection is from you

Under your umbrella I walk
You're saving me from the storm
Protecting me from the rain

For I no longer have to shield myself
You have an umbrella for me
Holding it when I don't feel able

You protect me
You stop the waters from washing me out
You are with me as I wander in the rain

I can now skip under your umbrella like a child
again
Sing your praises despite the conditions
For it is you who holds it up

God's Love

Love
A word we hear frequently
Told by many

An emotion
We feel often

We can love people
We can even love things

But there is love here
That at times we struggle to fathom

To put it simply
God loves you

It's not like any other love

Human love
often has conditions around it

But God's love
That's unconditional

Sometimes it's hard to accept this love
We feel we are not enough
We are not worthy

None of the above is true
as you accept the love of Christ things begin to
change

The love of God is not dependent on how you've
acted,
your past

It's just there
regardless of anything

We only have to look at the cross to see this is
true

Gods love is

Eternal love
True affection
Love without conditions
An absolute devotion

A glimpse of light in the darkness

Pitch black
No light in sight
Heavy clouds of grey
Weighing on your shoulders

Feeling lost
Abandoned
Frightened
Helpless

Along comes the light
A gentle illumination
Touching you
God has arrived

His grace pouring over you
His touch tender and kind
Don't be afraid he says
See my light

He takes your hand
Guides you through the darkness

Whisking you away
Into his loving arms

He is the glimpse of light
That you cannot miss
The one that comes running
In times of desperate need

I praise you

I praise you
I praise you on days where my heart aches
I praise you
I praise you when I'm in pain

For you lord,
Are so praiseworthy
Your faithfulness is never ending
Your love immeasurable

I praise you
I praise you for the blessings
I praise you
I praise you for the miracles

Jesus Christ,
You died on the cross for me
You came back
You forgive me of my sins

I praise you
I praise you for your promises
I praise you
I praise you that I'm never alone

At times,
I can't see you working
But my thankfulness
It will never stop

I praise you
I praise you for giving me life
I praise you
I praise you for every day

I lift up my hands
Shout your name in glory
Reach my hands higher
Thank you lord

Answered Prayers

Each morning,
I come to the father with a prayer,
Sometimes more than two

I come with an expectant heart
Hoping he will hear my request
And honour it

It is in God's timing
That I see
The answers of his prayers

He hears
He sees
He answers

Sometimes not in the way we hope
We are left disheartened,
disappointed

But God's faithfulness is clear
His steadfast love is evident
He waits until we are ready

Our father answers,

He brings us blessing after blessing
Healing

It may take time
But those answers will appear
He gives us more than we could ever hope for

Open your eyes
Open your heart
Receive your answered prayers

Swept Away

Life can be distracting
Society pulls us in different directions
Too easy to get swept away

Tv,
Social media
The news
The list is endless

So often I hear myself say:
I don't have time
I'm too tired
I'll do it later

Let me ask you this
Does our father ever say these things?
Does he feel too tired or too busy to talk?

Our hearts know
He longs for our prayers
For those late night chats about our woes

He wants to hear from you
He wants to know you
And he delights in you

The next time your favourite soap is on
Stop,
Be reminded of you creator

Stop
Remember the holy one
Stop
 turn back to him

Be still
Be still in his presence
Soak up his spirit
And rest in his arms